John MacDonald

Business Success

What it Is and How to Secure it

John MacDonald

Business Success
What it Is and How to Secure it

ISBN/EAN: 9783337310547

Printed in Europe, USA, Canada, Australia, Japan

Cover: Foto ©Suzi / pixelio.de

More available books at **www.hansebooks.com**

BUSINESS Success:

what it is and

how to secure it.

.

A LECTURE

.

DELIVERED BEFORE THE TORONTO YOUNG MEN'S
CHRISTIAN ASSOCIATION,

BY

JOHN MACDONALD

TORONTO:
ADAM, STEVENSON & CO.
1872.

TO

THE YOUNG MEN

OF OUR

DOMINION,

—ITS BUSINESS MEN TO BE,—

THIS LITTLE VOLUME IS DEDICATED

WITH THE

BEST WISHES OF THEIR FRIEND

THE AUTHOR.

·

PREFACE.

I had promised to deliver a lecture for the Young Men's Christian Association of this city in the early part of last year, on "Business Success." Duties, many and pressing, prevented my fulfilling that engagement earlier than last month. Many who heard it then, (including business men, in whose judgment I have much confidence), and others who heard of it, expressed a wish that it might be published.

The thoughts contained in it have been gathered from observation during the many years of an active business life. It will not be considered presumptuous then, if even the writer should think that their study will prove of service to the man of business, while the young man about setting out in life, (whatever his calling), cannot but be benefitted by their perusal.

It may be said that there are causes which lead, not only to success, but to failure, which are unnoticed here ; this, I admit; but the reader will remember that the matter was prepared not with the view of furnishing an exhaustive treatise on so important a subject, but as a lecture only, within which nothing more could be pressed than would interest an audience for a reasonable length of time.

Enough will be found, however, if carefully read and duly acted upon, to guard from failure ;—enough to point the way to a successful business career.

I have preferred, in this small volume, making no additions to the manuscript. This will make it more welcome to those who have but little time for reading, and none the less to those who have most.

The book, I trust, will have the effect of leading to a higher standard of commercial morality ; of deterring some from entering business whose talents fit them for other callings ; of inspiring others with high resolves to battle bravely and to win; and of leading all to acknowledge that God is seen in commerce as He is in every part of His vast universe; and that without His blessing, " it is vain to rise up early, to sit up late, to eat the bread of sorrows."

J. McD.

Oaklands, Toronto June, 1872.

BUSINESS SUCCESS.

I T has been affirmed that the majority of business men fail at some period of their career : that not more than five out of every hundred succeed. Both statements are startling; and yet neither should be hastily dismissed without careful examination. Whatever differences of opinion there may be about the first, we are inclined to think that experience will fully confirm the second.

There are no changes so great in any country as those found among its business men. Nor any calling is there, or profession, which yields so small a measure of success as business, in proportion to the numbers engaged. You find Judges on the Bench and Lawyers at the Bar, you find others actively engaged in their professions for ten, twenty, and thirty years. Not so with business men : you look for old familiar faces and they are gone. As you pass along the streets you find, instead of well known names, those of strangers, and before you are well familiar with them they disappear to give place to others. Think of the men in our own city, who not only sat upon our Bench, but adorned it; whose opinions were respected not only at home, but beyond it; think of those who in Law and Medicine took the very first place in their professions; men of mark, whose names became household words, and who engaged in active duties to the last, passed away full of years, and full of honours; and then look back, if you will, and count the number and tell the names of your successful business men of the same period. You will find but few, nor will you be able, we think, to make the average of those who succeed, more than five per cent.

Take up a Directory of this city which will carry you back twenty or thirty years : look for the names of the business men of those days : they have disappeared! You will be struck in finding the number who have been unsuccessful; but great as the number is, do not think it greater than that found in other cities of the same population : there is not a town or hamlet on this continent, which does not furnish the same results. The story of the majority of business men is, that they have been unsuccessful. But some will say: Canada is too small a field to form a fair estimate of the proportion of successful business men. Take a wider one: look at the United States! We venture to assert, without having examined the figures, that not five per cent. of the merchants of New York succeed. Quite likely says one: American merchants generally, are little better than a set of sharpers. Not so. There is no higher type of business men to be found than the high-toned American merchant.

That there are unprincipled traders in the United States, we think quite possible ; but have we not this class among ourselves ? We cannot see the propriety in any man bringing a sweeping charge against the business men of any country, simply because his transactions may have been (perhaps from choice) with the least reliable of its traders. Equally unsafe would it be to form our judgment from the verdict of those who complain only because they found themselves less skilled in the sharp practices of trade, than the sharper men into whose hands they fell. Some of the most advanced men of the day are business men, foremost in every good work ; with views too broad, sympathies too noble, and souls too great to suffer them to do anything small, mean, or contemptible;—whose princely incomes afford them ample opportunities of originating and executing benevolent schemes on a large scale. Such men are found in every land to-day, but in none do you find finer specimens, or in none do you find a larger proportion, than in the United States. Yet, take the city of New York in the year 1871 : it had three hundred and twenty-four failures, with liabilities amounting to $20.740.000. In the United States the failures for 1871 were 2915, with liabilities $85.252.000 ; in 1870, 3551, with liabilities $89.242.000; while in 1861, the liabilities were $207.000.000 ; and in 1857, over $291,000.000. These figures I know are very startling, and many will at once say that they must represent a loss to creditors *far beyond* anything, in proportion, which exists in Canada. Let us see. From 1864 to 1869, a period of a little over four years, there were in this Dominion, three thousand three hundred and thirty-two Insolvents, sufficient with their families to people a city ; and with liabilities sufficient to build it substantially, to adorn it with squares, fountains, handsome public buildings, churches and schools. Look at Ontario, this favoured province, not in a year of scarcity, but in a year of plenty,—in the most prosperous year of its history ; one might well say': *surely there were no failures!* We learn from the *Monetary Times* that there were three hundred and twenty-eight, with liabilities probably not under $5.000.000. Each number of the Ontario *Gazette* contains the notice of new Insolvents. In the issue of the last week of February, were notices of twenty-six. Assuming that to be a high weekly average, take the number at seven ; and you would then have not less than three hundred and sixty-four Insolvents per annum. We find in a paper of the Province of Quebec, dated February 29th, the notices of twelve Insolvents for that Province : this only a local paper in a period of not more than seventeen days ; and for such notices in each of the Provinces we may look with as much certainty as we look for the spring-time and the autumn. If this be so, one is ready to inquire : Is it safe to go into business ? Is it wisdom to adopt a calling which has so few prizes and so many blanks ? If business to so many means disaster and bankruptcy ; if men of good ability, moderate capital, and fair prospects, have long battled, and yet in the end have had all swept away, how, I would ask, is it possible that I can travel that road and escape its dangers ?— navigate that ocean, and pass safely through its storms?— fight that battle, and not fight only—but win. It would be a good thing not only for those engaged in trade, but for the entire community who share, more or less, in the sufferings and loss which failures bring, if each man beginning business would propose these questions to himself, or to some one upon whose judgment he could rely ;—a good thing if he would insist upon an honest and faithful reply. The result would be, that thirty per cent. of all the men who go into business would discover that there were other fields in which they could better distinguish themselves ; callings for which their talents were more suited, and which, though promising to bring with them greater labour, would also bring to them greater reward. And yet although trade has its risks, uncertainties and failures, there is no need that business men should be unsuccessful. True, there are dangers, but men may escape them. There are laurels to be won, and men may win and wear them, as having been fairly and bravely won.

It is possible that one's business career may be one of unbroken triumph; possible to reach a first-class commercial position, while friends will delight and foes, if men have them, will be compelled to acknowledge that they who have honourably attained it are successful business men.

Some regard business as a lottery ; others as a game of chance, in which none but the fortunate win ; others tell you that tricks are a necessary part of trade, that everything in business is fair, even over-reaching and untruthfulness ; and, that without these, success is impossible. It is time that all such ideas were swept away, for they are dangerous, misleading and untrue.

That there may be found untruthful and over-reaching men in business, we are ready to admit; and because such men may have accumulated means in business by cunning, or possibly by fraud, there are those who have conceived that success in business is to be secured only by such methods.

The proportion which our unsuccessful traders bear to our successful ones is so large that we are not surprised that many should regard business as a lottery, and conclude that while here and there one may find a successful business man, yet, that the great majority must fail. These are all mistakes. There are certain business principles which, if strictly and constantly followed, will as surely result in business success, as that a vessel by careful navigation can be safely brought to her destination, or that brave troops, skillfully handled by a brave general, may be led to victory. Failure is not necessarily a part of business, nor must it be concluded that fifty or even ten out of every hundred men who go into business must fail. I know that to the most honourable, failure is possible; men have been ruined in their efforts to save others : just as many a bold swimmer has been pulled down by a drowning man whose life he sought to save. The fire will desolate on land; ships will go down at sea; markets will drop suddenly; occasionally there

will be a shrinkage of values; bills of Exchange will be
returned; banks will fail; and thus men, honest and
well-intentioned, will sometimes find themselves compelled to ask the consideration of their creditors; and
although in such cases there may have been a lack of
becoming prudence, yet these remarks are needed to
rescue such men from the odium which so often is connected with failure, and to save them from being classed
either as fools or knaves. Making full allowance, however,
for such cases, we contend that ninety per cent. of our
failures might be avoided: and that business might be a
certain instead of an uncertain thing; that disaster might
be the exception and not the rule. There is no need that
men should break down in early life, as the result of
continued business perplexity. No need that homes
should be made sad and cheerless, through business
difficulties, which ought always to be happy and
cheerful;—no need that business which a wise Providence designed should be the means of contributing so largely to the comfort and happiness
of the human family in every part of the world, should be
the cause to so many of misery and ruin: business may
be stripped of nine-tenths of the doubt which now sur-
rounds it and men may see with some confidence, when
they begin a business career that they will be able to
bring it to a prosperous and successful close.

Nearly six thousand of our seamen are drowned every year, as the returns to Parliament for 1870 show! Apart from the brave sailors who thus annually perish, how many are there who go down to the sea in ships, either on business or pleasure, who find every year a watery grave. That this waste of life is no necessary part of travelling by sea, is abundantly proved by the long and prosperous career of the Cunard company. True, they have lost seamen and may yet lose more. Men will in a fool-hardy way, expose their lives by sea as well as by land; but during thirty years and more, from the first trip of their first steamship to the present hour, every passenger who has not imprudently exposed his life or died from natural causes, has been safely landed at his destination. Nor has a letter or a parcel been lost through the negligence of the company. Their vessels have been in every storm ; have borne the rage of every hurricane which has swept over the ocean during these long years ;—mid rain and fog, and sleet and ice ; watchful and careful, they have carried their passengers with greater safety than those passengers could have travelled on land by any conveyance, and have fairly won the high reputation they enjoy to-day, by a management in the navigation of ocean steamships the most perfect and the most successful, the world has ever known.

The bungling of the Crimea was the real enemy our brave soldiers had to contend with. Want of food, clothing, tents, and even fuel, in the depth of a Crimean winter, soon produced their results :—exhaustion, fever, cholera, and trench work wrought among them far greater havoc than did the fire of the enemy.

The Expedition to Abyssinia proved that misman-agement, endangering the lives or even the health of troops, is no necessary part of a military campaign ; that it is possible to lead an army through a country, the difficulties of which are vastly greater than those of the Crimea with perfect safety ; that commissariat arrange-ments and sanitary regulations can be made so perfect, that men need not suffer for lack of food, clothing, tents or fuel, and that the health of the troops may be main-tained at as high an average as if they were stationed at Aldershot, or, better still, at the garrison in Toronto.

So with business. Thousands fail every year, but they need not. The fact that men live through the same crisis which swept them away, is proof that they might have done the same. That men have lived through many crises in which men stronger financially than they were, have been ruined, and that though some of these storms have been terribly severe, have nobly braved them

all, not perhaps with capital unimpaired ; but with credit
unaffected, and with character untarnished. Men, who,
guided by lofty principle, scorned the idea of taking ad- .
vantage of a panic to propose a compromise ; never
asked what was expedient, but what was right ; whose
bark when the rage of the tempest was past, was found
at anchor ; a spar or two gone, perhaps a little battered,
but still at anchor ; while here, and there, and yonder, lay
stranded and broken wrecks in wild and shapeless confu-
sion. That such men could outride such storms is enough
to prove that others could do the same, and that it is no
more necessary for a man to fail because he goes into
business than it is for a man to be drowned because he
goes to sea.

But why, it may be asked, have the Cunard company been so successful ? All that can be obtained in
human skill and ingenuity is brought to bear in the con-
struction of their vessels ; everything about their ships
must be of the very best. The ship itself, its machinery,
charts, compasses, stearing gear ; officers tried and capable, brave and daring ; yet, cool and cautious ; en-
gineers, men high up in their profession ; crews, the best
that can be secured. In their passages the first consideration is safety ; the second, speed ; the third, profit.
Is it any wonder that they have been so successful.

Some of our volunteers thought the medical examination of the force designed for the Red River expedition unnecessarily severe. Had every man who deemed himself fit to undergo its hardships been allowed to form part of the force, many would have gone, who would have hindered rather than helped it. It was deemed best that the force should be formed only of men of strong and sound constitutions. Their way lay through an unknown and uninhabited wilderness, where it might fairly be expected there would be formidable obstacles to meet which would require all the strength and endurance of healthy and powerful men. The successful completion of that expedition, without a single casualty, shows how wise were these precautions ; and how perfect was the organization.

Let business men have the same fitness for their calling as our Canadian volunteers of the Red River expedition had for theirs ; the same enthusiasm as these brave fellows had in entering upon the difficulties of that unknown and unexplored way ; the same care, the same caution, which the Cunard company have exercised during their lengthened career, and you will have the same successful results. Let it be understood that a business man requires something more than friends, or means, though both are excellent ; and it is difficult to get on without either. That if he lacks character, it matters little what else he may have. That he wants brains and common sense, for many a man has the one, who lacks the other. That he wants business fitness, and a confidence that leads him to look upon difficulties as playthings,—to think, and speak, and believe in nothing but success. In one word, have in business as elsewhere, always the right man in the right place. Then the number of your successful men will be immensely increased, and a commercial crisis a matter of rare occurrence.

Success is possible in a bad cause as well as in a good one ; yet we understand by the word, the favourable or prosperous termination of anything attempted for purposes of profit or improvement. Business is a word of such extensive and indefinite signification, that it may be applied with great propriety in describing the occupation of many who are not engaged in trade. We look at it only from its mercantile aspect.

What measure of those qualities which make great business men is inherited and what acquired, we do not undertake to determine ; whether a man can become a business man of high order, who is not born a merchant we leave others to decide.

When Peabody, in 1856 went to Danvers to revisit the scenes of his childhood and to receive the honours which his fellow townsmen were anxious to offer, he said :—

"Though Providence has granted me unvaried, and unusual success, in the pursuit of fortune in other lands ; I am still in heart the humble boy who left yonder unpretending dwelling. There is not a youth within the sound of my voice, whose early opportunities and advantages are not very much greater than were my own, and I have since achieved nothing that is impossible to the most humble boy among you."

The modesty of Peabody led him to speak thus, but he was mistaken. Great business ability, such as he possessed, is not profusely bestowed. A man who stood in the very first rank among the merchant princes of London ; who in trade won laurels as many and as proud as they ; who became the benefactor not only of the country of his birth, but of that of his adoption ; who received marks of distinguished favour from the President of the United States, and to whom the Queen of England presented her own portrait specially prepared for him upon a plate of pure gold, must have been a man among many thousands ; and every boy whom he addressed could no more become a merchant like Peabody than he could become a general like Wellington, or an engineer like Stephenson. Aim high, be ambitious to take the first business position ; but do not be surprised if you fail to reach the lofty position of Peabody, and men of his class, and do not be discouraged ; for we know that there are positions which if not nearly as influential as that held by him ; wealth, which if not nearly as great as he possessed ; credit which if not nearly as extensive as he enjoyed ; yet, once obtained, would entitle you or any one to be regarded in this or any land as a *successful business man.*

You cannot form a correct estimate of a man's business success by mere outward appearances. The ambition to make a social flourish upon inadequate means is not only an evil, but a growing one, and many are led to mistake outside glitter for accumulated wealth. It would be as unsafe to judge of a man's success by the outward flash he makes, as it would be to estimate the value of the mine by mere surface indications. You will be told, if you would rightly judge of the value of the mine, you must test it below the surface ; and the banker will tell you that in his parlour, you will find a better picture of a man's business position than you can possibly get from mere outward appearances. There are those who pay

homage to wealth,—men are courted for their means ;—
yet great means do not always imply great business
ability.

Some acquire a reputation for business ability and
success to which they have no claim ; their ability con-
sisting merely in inheriting the large means employed in
their business. Others by monopolies or restrictions acquire the control of articles of trade solely for their own
enrichment, to the loss, and ruin, perhaps, of other
trades. Legislative acts have been framed, tariffs en-
acted, legislators corrupted, for no other purpose than to
secure such monopolies for individuals or corporations.
What matter though coal be put beyond the reach of the
poor, so that they are enriched ; and equally regardless
are they of the disturbance which the increased price of
any commodity may create so long as the result is turned
to their profit; and then men look at the immense palaces
the fruit of such gains, and call their owners successful
business men. Such men are mere adventurers and their
gains the results of bribery, corruption and fraud. Equally
unsafe would it be to regard the very rapid acquirement
of means in every case as a test of business success. If
so the most successful men of our time have been the
members of the Tammany Ring. For no men ever made
money more rapidly, and if all be true, none ever made

it more dishonestly. Wealth acquired through long years of honourable business life is an evidence of success ; and where with great wealth you find a great heart, and great enjoyment in the right use of means, you have the finest type of a successful business man. Yet to great wealth we must not attach undue importance ; for how many do we find who having enormous means, are nevertheless miserable, mean, and poor. True "The hand of the diligent maketh rich." We may have deligence and its reward, and yet the man himself may be utterly incapable of turning to any useful account the means he has acquired. Some hoard large means from no other motive it would appear, than to have men say of them that they *died rich*. Such men may have piled away in chests thousands of gold and silver, but for all the good their gold is likely to do themselves or others, they might as well have so many stones. Such men live in daily fear of burglars and skeleton keys, of banks breaking, of commercial ruin ; of such, and there are many everywhere, one is ready to say : "there is more hope of a fool than of him." There is no young man in this assembly, who, while in a respectable situation, enjoying life as he passes through it ; has confidence in his fellow men, is bright, cheerful, and hopeful, though he may not be possessed of fifty dollars, who could exchange places with such a man without being an immense loser.

2

Wealth that has been acquired by ruining manufac-
terers, underpaying employees, and bringing about the
failure of weak competitors, cannot bring pleasure. For
the thought will obtrude itself even amid the splendour of
establishments so secured, as one looks at their ships
or palaces, that they have been secured by oppression,
injustice and wrong. We do not see that you can form a
fair estimate of a man's success by looking at him apart
from his destiny. He may count his gold by millions,
but gold does not bring happiness. Where men live to
accumulate it for its own sake, and toil for it so as to forget that they have a hereafter, it becomes not only a
snare, but a curse, and it would have been better for such
men had they lived and died poor. It was once asked
of such an one : " How much did he leave ?" " Every
dollar," was the quick and suitable reply. "He took none
with him." Where there are no correct views of a man's
responsibility ; where there is neither desire nor heart to
use means rightly, enormous wealth simply means enormous anxiety ; accumulation instead of bringing content-
ment only creates the desire for more ; a bondage the
most cruel, a thirst for wealth which refuses to be satisfied ;
and as millions are added to the already enormous pile, the
cry is still : more! more ! Richer and happier by far, and
more useful to the world, is he who, satisfied with mod-
est means, enjoys the fruit of his labours. Nor is there

one here who having the choice of positions, but would
choose the latter—

> Who only asks for humblest wealth ;
> Enough for competence and health,
> And leisure when the day is done ;
> > To read his book by chimney nook,
> > Or stroll at setting of the sun.
> Who toils as every man should toil:
> For fair reward, erect and free,—
> These are the men, the best of men,
> These are the men we mean to be.

" Better is a handful with quietness, than both hands
full, with travail and vexation of spirit."

Gold, I know, is with many the measure of a man's
success. If it has cost him the loss of health, produced an enfeebled frame, or weakened intellect, what has
he gained ? If it has made him a grub worm, and kept
him ever looking with his eyes fixed on the earth so that
he had neither pleasure or desire to look up at the bright
blue sky ; if while it has led him to be thickly lining his
pockets, has also led him to neglect the cultivation and
enrichment of his mind, so that he is bankrupt in every
thing but gold, whatever measure of success the world
may award him as a business man, he has been an immense loser. Should his application bring upon him
suffering as it is likely to do, so that he become an in-

valid ; or should he be spared to reach old age, which to such an one would certainly bring its infirmities ; he would be found a poor man without the resources which would enable him to endure the one state, or without the cheerfulness which is the charm of the other. While he who through life has felt that neither the pressure nor the emoluments of business could lead him to neglect the garnishing of his mind, draws to its close with richly stored resources within himself, which render age not only endurable but delightful, who as he thinks

> "On years that time has cast behind,
> But reaps delight from toil and pain."
>
> "As when the transient storm is past,
> The sudden gloom and driving shower,
> The sweetest sunshine is the last,
> The loveliest is the evening hour."

He is a successful man who meets all his obligations with promptness, and who for his business has a " rest " sufficient to meet all its contingencies ; whose name stands high in the first commercial circles ; whose judgment and counsel is sought and respected, and whose whole course is above suspicion and worthy of imitation ; whose business is ever in such a state that, if removed by death, enough will be found to discharge every obligation, and enough remain for those dependent upon him.

He is the most successful who, in addition to the capital employed in his business, has means and time to do good with them ; whose life, in the best sense, is a busy one; who makes money not only by his fellow-men, but for them ; who enjoys life as he passes through it ; who, though in business, is a busy man ; is, in the best sense, a busy worker who is watchful to improve those opportunities where his means, influence and experience enable him to do most good.

"Nations become rich and powerful by the continued and well-protected efforts of individuals to improve their condition and rise in the world. The labour and the savings of all such are at once the source and the measure of national opulence and public prosperity."

To the humblest we may then say :

" Hold up your brow in honest pride ;
Though rough and swarth yours hands may be,
Such hands are sap-veins that provide
The life-blood of the nation's tree."

What are the causes of failure ?

The first we notice is *Incompetency.* Hundreds of men go into business in Canada, and we presume elsewhere, who, for everything connected with its management, are thoroughly incompetent : clergymen with sore throats, school-masters who find confinement oppressive, farmers who tell you that their work is laborious; mechanics who think "keeping store," as they term it, more respectable than their own trade ; now and then a stray doctor ; and although there are those in each of these classes who succeed, they do so mainly from a force of character which would equally well serve them in any other pursuit.

If you wanted a book bound, you would not be likely to send it to a carpenter; nor, if you wanted a broken leg set, would you be likely to send for a tin-smith. Would it not be well for doctors, clergymen and mechanics, who think that without any training they possess a thorough fitness for business, to remember that years of application were needed to fit them for the duties of the callings they are throwing aside ; that without such preparation they would have been unable to have sustained themselves as they had hitherto done, and that some training at least would be required for the business they are about to attempt. It is simply cruel to encourage such men to go into a business with the simplest details of which they are utterly ignorant ; cruel to take from them the earnings of years when it is quite apparent that the end can only be disaster ; entering upon a business of which they know nothing, to be left behind in a race for which they are altogether unequal ; to become the victim of some unprincipled trader, or to fritter their means away through sheer incompetency and to find out, when too late, that they had no fitness for business and should never have attempted it.

Eighty per cent. of our failures are the result of *Extravagance.*

Don't be startled ; that will be found to be under, rather than over the mark. Extravagance is a disease which, though in some admitting of treatment, in others is incurable. There are some who act, as soon as they have obtained a credit, as though their fortune had been made. Their business and home expenses, assume proportions of an unwarranted nature ; nor do they pause to consider whether such expenditure can be long maintained, or whether it is likely speedily to come to an end. Such men run their course in an incredibly short time. When the end comes, they call it imprudence. It is dishonesty, and nothing else. There are many men in business to-day, who are building houses, buying lands, and living in a reckless and extravagant style, on the strength of a credit obtained for strictly business purposes.

There are others who fail through extravagance, but do so more slowly ; tempted first to indulge in some unwarranted expenditure, they resist for a while, perhaps, but then yield. The appetite for further expenditure becomes a craving one, and as it increases the ability to resist it diminishes. They wavered when they should have been firm, vaccilated when they should have resisted ; and from that hour their downward course began. Suppose a young man who has recently commenced business with moderate capital, good credit, and fair prospects. Things go on well. His wife, who knows little of business, but takes it for granted that he is doing well, puts in her claim, let us say for a piano. If he studied her happiness and his own, his answer would be : "Gladly, when we can afford it, and a piano stool, and a music stand, and anything else that we really require ; but we must wait patiently until it can be well afforded, without inconvenience to business, or without jeopardizing the means of others."

Do not think that I suppose an improbable case. There are few failures which take place in the country where you will not find a piano among the household furniture, and as a matter of course, you are always told that it belongs to the wife.

Now, he is the best husband who can talk to his wife in this way, and she the best wife who, fully appre-

ciating his motives, is contented with such a reply ; and each so denying themselves, in due time husband and wife will be abundantly rewarded. But the man yields, the piano is bought, for he says he can get this bill renewed. Then the carpets look shabby, and they must get new ones. The furniture is old-fashioned, and the curtains are faded, and when the first step is taken it is the simplest matter to glide into others equally uncalled for. Then follow the neglect of business ; the accumulation of bills ; the protesting of notes ; the stoppage of credit ; the loss of confidence ; the meeting of creditors ; the visit of the sheriff's officer; piano gone, carpets and curtains gone ; the man broken-spirited, broken-hearted. The morning that shone out so promising, already dark and beclouded. Then, in too many instances, the bottle,—then the grave.

Hundreds of men are ruined through *Intemperance.* When a man finds that he requires stimulants to give him the energy needed for his business, he is in a bad way. When you find men stand back from you in conversation, or turn their heads away from you lest you should discover their habits, they are in a dangerous position. When you find them constantly dull, dreamy, and stupid, make up your mind, if you are a creditor, that unless there be a speedy and radical change, you may look forward to a bad debt, and to the man's destruction.

In Great Britain, where a very large amount of business is transacted by travelling, thousands of young men and their customers have been ruined by the drinking usages of the road. [A young man who is a commercial traveller need not be a drinker. Nor need he, to sell goods, offer drink to others. We would be glad if the commercial travellers of our young Dominion and their customers would alike set their face against an evil which has already slain so many bright, promising young men, and desolated so many happy homes, and shew to the same class in the Old World that here they can do business upon its own merits, and are opposed to practices which, though having the appearance of present profit, are but sowing the seed which can bring forth nothing but ruin and death.

Many fail through *Speculation.* They see those who through long years of patient industry have acquired position, influence and means, and whose trials, by the way, they know nothing of; and despising the slow but certain paths of their own business (the safest at all times), enter into some wild and reckless undertaking by which they expect to make a fortune immediately. Others, they are told, have tried the same thing, but they were stupid, had no business talent, had not seized the right time—*were fools.* Upon such men words and arguments are wasted ; it is folly to talk to them of meeting bills, either with the banker or wholesale dealer ; they hope to be bankers or wholesale dealers themselves within six months. There is an oil property, and in the venture there is a perfect mint of money. There are a few shares to be had in some joint-stock company, which will yield immense returns, and they are to be had at par. Or a village has just been mapped out in the wilderness, or is going to be, and the place is destined to become one of the most important cities on the continent, and they intend to secure a large number of the lots. And so with a thousand things ; some of them as ridiculous as the bogus companies of the South Sea Bubble days.

. There is extant a list of nearly two hundred bubble companies started in the year of bubbles, none of which were under £1,000,000, and some went as far as £10,000,000, stg. One was designed to make salt water fresh ; another to furnish merchants with watches ; a third to discover perpetual motion ; a fourth to plant mulberry trees and breed silk-worms in Chelsea park ; a fifth, to import large jackasses from Spain in order to propagate a larger kind of mule in England ; while an advertisement was issued that at a certain place "on Tuesday next, books will be opened for a subscription of £2,000,000, for the invention of melting sawdust and chips and casting them into clean deal boards, without cracks and without knots." Not less ridiculous are some of the schemes into which men rush to-day,—with means not their own, but entrusted to them only for legitimate business purposes, bringing upon others loss, perhaps suffering, and stamping themselves for all time to come as dangerous men whom it would be unsafe to trust.

We have no "Wall Street" here, and we are glad of it. Many of its brokers to-day are but wrecks of what were once thrifty business men. Tempted to try their hand at some fancy stock, they listened in an evil hour, were led on step by step, until they lost property, business habits, friends, all. Henry Ward Beecher recently delivered a lecture on "Wall Street." He stated that he had buried from it, in a period of twenty-five years, four generations of men. He says it is a dunghill of mushrooms; there is in it every year a vast growth of men, and every year they are trampled down in hosts. "I know," he says, "but one or two men in that period who have been able to make permanent gains; nor was this done by speculation; they added other means of accumulation which were the foundation of their stability."

Profanity and *Sabbath-breaking* bring about commercial disaster. They are presented together, for they are inseparable. We have no confidence in the success of either a profane man or a Sabbath-breaker; nor have we any confidence in the future of the young man who is either the one or the other. Nothing, to business men, is of greater moment than the confidence of creditors; this class of traders may impress men so as to secure their confidence, but they will retain it not one day after their habits are known. The command to labour for six days is as imperative as that which enjoins rest upon the seventh; and while a blessing is promised to those who diligently labour during the six days, it is promised only in connection with the proper observance and rest of the seventh. When men tell you they are so closely confined during the week, and have to work so hard that the only church they can get to is the country—the only minister they can hear, Dr. Greenfields—you may mark them, for sooner or later *they will fail.* Some there are who, belonging to none of these classes, fall behind from positive inability to keep up with younger and more active competitors. To use a common phrase, they get "behind the age," and others, from circumstances of a nature peculiar to their own case, and without intention to defraud, bring upon themselves disaster, and for which they feel as deeply, perhaps more so, than the creditors to whom they occasion loss.

Although failures are of regular occurrence, it is in the crisis when they come thick and fast. And then wise ones shake their heads and gravely tell you that they saw it coming ; that it has been caused by excessive importation, injudicious credits, reckless over-trading, and a continued contraction of the money market. All these causes, we take it, exist more or less in every crisis, for they are certain, sooner or later, to produce commercial disturbance. But these wise people find this out just when every one else finds it out—when it is too late. Raise the standard of your business men, let fitness and character be regarded as indispensable to the obtainment of credit, let the honest trader feel that his competition is to be only with honest traders, and the crisis will be something less to be feared, and the assets of commercial men will represent a value they do not now possess.

The merchants of Tyre were princes, her trafficers the honourable of the earth ; her sails were spread to every breeze, the sound of her oars heard in every sea. When her wares went forth she filled many people, and enriched the kings of the earth. Of the prophet Ezekiel's description of her wealth, beauty, influence, and far-reaching commerce, it has been said that for graphic power, high poetic imagery, and historic accuracy of detail,

the passage is unequalled in the whole compass of litera-
ture. What a commentary her history presents of the
changes which take place, not only with great commercial men, but with great commercial centres. When we
remember that she who, in the days of her glory, "heaped
up riches as the dust, and fine gold as the mire of the
streets," is to-day but a scene of ruins and of the deepest
poverty, upon whose fallen ramparts the fisherman spreads
his nets; when it is remembered that her towers, her
temples, her palaces, her harbour, her commerce, her
wealth and her glory, are all things of the past, how can
one help exclaiming, "What city is like Tyrus, like the
destroyed in the midst of the sea !"

It would be pleasant to trace the development of
commerce from its decline among the Phœnicians to the
present period, when the trade of the British Islands has
attained a magnitude never reached before in the history
of the world; but such a subject would take us beyond
our limits. Let us say, however, that if Tyre had her
merchant princes, so has Great Britain; that if the honourable of the earth were the trafficers of the one, so are
they of the other. But Britain has a glory which Tyre
never knew. Her chief city, which needed not Mac-
aulay's unborn artist of New Zealand to render famous—
while it is the centre of the nation's trade—is the centre

of the nation's charity. It is undoubtedly a great honour to be Lord Mayor of London, (an office usually held by one of London's merchant princes), but perhaps the chief attraction of the office consists in the fact that the Lord Mayor is the great almoner of the nation. No spot is there where the cry of suffering or oppression is heard more readily than in the Mansion House ; none is there from which help comes so quickly or so munificently. Whether the cry come from the beleaguered Parisians, dying by thousands from exhaustion and famine ; from Persia, in the low moans of famishing men ; from gory battle-fields where, side by side, those who, but a few hours before, were deadly foes, have been made friends by reason of their common suffering ; or from the homeless thousands of Chicago, as they stand amid the ruins of their charred and blackened city—the great heart of the English people is moved. No question is asked in reference to faith, colour or government. It is enough to know that there is suffering, and that it cries for help. The one broad, strong tie of human brotherhood is all that is needed to call forth the splendid offerings of Britain's princely merchants; and food and raiment, and gold and silver, are poured forth with a princely generosity, which, while it meets the wants of the suffering, calls forth the admiration of the world.

I am aware that it has been sneeringly said of Great Britain that she is a nation of shopkeepers ; yet where do you find such a nation, and where do you find such shopkeepers ? To such princely merchants we point you, and ask you to imitate their example if you would enjoy like success.

To succeed in business, one should have a strong preference for it, amounting to a passion ; should possess a fitness for it, should be early and well trained in a good school. It is questionable whether any man ever made his mark in business, who did not, as a boy, exhibit a strong liking for it. A passion as great as that which led Philip to forget the glazing of the windows, as he stood in rapture gazing at the paintings ; which found Flaxman pencilling at six, Stephenson modelling engines in clay while a child, Sir Christopher Wren evincing his preference for mechanics, and Nelson that love of bold adventure, and that happy unconsciousness of fear, which gave promise of his splendid and brilliant career. These all became great men ; their names and their deeds are part of their nation's history ; nor will either be forgotten so long as our language is spoken, or time endure.

Budgett was born a merchant. At the age of ten, when on his way to school, Arthur, his biographer, tells

3

us he found a horse-shoe; he carried it three miles and sold it to a blacksmith for a penny. That, he says, was his first penny. He kept it for some time. He found, while at school, that while a halfpenny would purchase six marbles, for a penny he could buy fourteen. At once he began to traffic in marbles; he bought in the larger, and sold in the smaller qantities. He next buys a quantity of cucumbers, upon which he clears ninepence; when he had two shillings and sixpence he bought a young jackass, this he sold to a Mrs. Ellis for five shillings. (You see he looked for respectable profits). Mrs. Ellis had no money, but she had a pair of new stays, which cost her ten shillings; these he took as collateral security. Meantime the donkey died, and Mrs. Ellis demanded her stays. He contended that the donkey died through ill-treatment, and refused to return them. These incidents exhibit the amazing passion for trade in a lad of tender years, and to some extent furnish us with the secret of his successful life. Budgett, in many respects, is not our model, although Arthur has written his life with much ability, and we commend its perusal to young men, assured that it will prove of service to them. There is one point, however, in the character of Budgett, which we cannot pass by without injustice to his memory and the subject we are treating. It is the point which we like most :—While not yet fifteen, he had made, by trading, thirty pounds ; the whole of this he gave to his parents, and although they purposed returning it to him, were never able to do so. I choose rather to find in this act the foundation of his fortune. While thoughtful men, as they look at the business bequeathed by him to his children, with its spacious warehouses, its hundreds of employees, its returns—estimated probably by millions —will not fail to trace a connection between these results and the act to which we have referred ; or call to remembrance the words spoken by the Saviour to the rich young man in the gospel, as conducive to his happiness in this world and the next : " Honour thy father and thy mother." We are not afraid of the success of the young man, whatever his calling, who honours his parents. Indeed we would not be afraid to predict it, while we would hesitate to pronounce favourably upon the future of him who, though having first-rate abilities, spoke lightly of his parents, or treated their counsels with indifference.

Parents often make grevious blunders in deciding upon the future of their children, simply because they have already determined in their own minds what their future callings shall be. How often do we hear parents speak of their children as though they had no will of their own, as though they would be equally successful in that calling for which they had a positive hatred, as in that to which they were most attached. Hence some parents say: "Our Tom is a sharp, cunning fellow, we are going to make him a lawyer." Another will say: "Chris. is so very quiet I am *afraid* we will have to make him a minister;" while a third says: "We are going to send Jack to his uncle's office and make him a merchant." It would be a good thing for the church and the world if there were fewer ministers who have been thus made, and it would be well for parents to wake up and learn that they can no more make their boys merchants than they can make them ministers.

There are boys who strongly desire to go to business, and their parents say "No," and, like Mrs. Swift, say to them, "You must be a lawyer." There are boys who want to be mechanics, and their parents say "*No*, you must go to business;" and as the result of this conflict between the will of the parents and the wish of the boys, we have briefless lawyers who would have made splendid business men, and we have unsuccessful business men who would have made splendid mechanics. Where the passion for a calling exists, you generally find the fitness for it; and where that fitness is wanting, it is the merest folly on the part of parents to urge their children to follow it. This pride on the part of parents, which leads them to fear that, if their boys go to business, they will rub against those of obscure birth, is something with which we have no patience, and can find no words to describe the contempt with which we regard it. It is time, not in this country alone, but everywhere, that the worth of men should be estimated, not so much by the accident of their birth, as by their character; time that it should be acknowledged that the son of a coal-heaver has as much right to aim at the best positions in the land, as the son of a lord, and securing which against great odds, is fairly entitled to wear the *honour* he wins. No man, however high his birth, standing side by side with such a man should feel other than honoured, for—

"Princes and lords are but the breath of kings :
'An honest man's the noblest work of God." '

The young man whose life is to be a business one, should begin its study early, prosecute it patiently, acquire it thoroughly. He should be at it not later than fifteen, and it will require all the application he is capable of giving it for the next ten years, to fit him for the responsible duties of a business life ; and away through the long years after, if he would be successful, he must still be learning. No young man ever succeeded who was afraid of work ; no young man ever will. The less his time and thoughts are exercised about tight-fitting kid gloves, flashy jewellery, and that exquisite style of "getting-up" so essential to the very existence of some young men, the better. The more ready he is to work, to work hard, and long, and willingly; the deeper the interest he takes in the business welfare of his employer; the more he throws his energies into his work; the more he is influenced in all that he does from principle; the more likely is he to succeed. When you see one taking as deep a concern in all that pertains to the interest of his employer as though the business were his own; whose zeal behind his master's back is of the same unflagging, steady character as when he is present, you may safely mark him; for, find him where you will, you will find one in whose word you can confide, and upon whose honour you can rely.

The advantages of being well trained in a good school cannot be over-estimated. Not one young man in every hundred, either in Canada or in the United States, learns his business as he would have to learn it in Great Britain. There, from five to seven years of close attention are thought necessary to prepare a man for business; but at the end of that time he has acquired it thoroughly, so that it will secure him a living in any part of the world, and fit him for taking the first commercial position.

Every man in the United States is eligible for the Presidency. It is not strange, therefore, that young men who have been twelve months in the packing room, should think themselves competent, in their own language, to "run the concern." Or that one who had been the same time in the warehouse, should think himself quite able to do the foreign buying. But in Canada, where ideas are more conservative, it is a matter of astonishment that young men are not more wishful to acquire that thorough groundwork, that mastery of their business, without which success is almost impossible. There must be a vast improvement in the business training of our young men, a greater attention to system and detail, a more thorough acquaintance with every department of business, before we can expect largely to increase the number of our successful business men.

We have spoken of the folly of parents urging their children to follow a calling for which they had no liking. We have before us the names of fifty young men, who, twenty-five or thirty years ago, went to business, some of them possibly to please their parents only. Their history will give us some idea of the uncertainties of a business life, and will show us also that it requires something more than a parent's wishes to make that business life a successful one :—Twenty-seven are dead and missing, three became ministers, two lawyers, one a physician, one a forwarder, one became deranged, seven are in situations. Of the fifty, eight have been in business on their own account, of these five have failed. Three are in business to-day, and occupy good positions as business men. If this should be thought a small proportion, it is only right to say, that as compared with business young men, of the present day, they were all fully up to, several of them much above the average.

It is a common thing to see iron steam-ships anchored in the Gare loch in the Frith of Clyde for several days before going to sea. The absence of magnetic disturbance has led to its selection as one of the best places for the testing of compasses.

Every young man who is about to commence business should first carefully examine whether he possesses those principles by which alone he can hope to steer. He is about to undertake a perilous journey, let him look well to his compasses. Begin well; not too young. Nothing is lost by waiting a few years. Years bring a maturity of thought and judgment, a knowledge of men and things, which no very young man can possibly possess; and which, once obtained, will be valuable beyond anything that can possibly be conceived by that restless young man whose only discipline has been hasty and imperfect. Experience in some cases is really more essential than capital,—without it no business can be conducted successfully. As it must be secured, it had better be acquired with patience than purchased by bitterness. Let no uneasy, restless promptings, no impatience to be your own master, lead you hastily to take a step not well and duly considered, not warranted by the circumstances of the hour, and the result of which you may have to regret, perhaps bitterly. You have much to learn : learn it well ; seize the proper time ; select your location wisely ; make good arrangements ; begin modestly. Do not attempt to do in one year what it has taken others twenty to accomplish. Your apparent gains may not be so large as those who aim at a trade questionable and hazardous, because altogether unwarranted by their means ; but what you make will be more certain. While you carry no more sail than you are able to manage in any storm, you secure the confidence of those whose confidence is your best capital, while those who crowd on all their canvass are ever in danger of shipwreck, and steadily impair the confidence of those who can best help them. You may be called a small buyer ; never mind, go on ; carefully and modestly, but go on : slow and sure is a good motto, for every young man commencing business, alike for himself and his creditors. Caution is always a safer element in a man's character than flash; nor do they who make "haste to be rich" accomplish the most good or prove the most successful. You will remember that in the long run, the tortoise beat the hare.

It has been said that the best way to secure peace is to be prepared for war. To secure business success guard against every possibility of failure. That you may be able to do this, you want the carefulness which avoids disaster, and the enthusiasm which knows of nothing but success. Be careful in your expenditure; not penurious or shabby,—but careful.

We have said that eighty per cent. of our failures. are the result of extravagance, we might add, of all the misery in the world, and yet if young men have not learned the secret of living within their means before they go into business, they are not likely to do so after. Many a young man, possessing fair business abilities, has found his way blocked in the obtainment of credit, and· has been astonished to find that men not nearly as well up as himself obtained support ; the merchant or banker to whom he applied, in making a fair estimate of his chance of success decided against him, and in favour of the other, who, though less showy was all the more sure. There is not an extravagant young man in this or any

city whose habits are not known, or who is likely to succeed so long as he continues them.

The prudence so essential, not only to a man's success
but to his happiness, is not learned at the bench of the
carpenter, the counting house of the merchant, or the
lawyer's office; it is learned at home. It is learned as
everything else that is good is learned : from one's mother.
And what a young man is when he leaves home, he is
likely to continue to the end. Is it too much to say
that no man becomes a great man who has not a great
mother. She may not be rich, she may not be of earth's
great ones, hers may be a lowly position, her few friends
humble as herself; she may, nevertheless, be great. Great
in the love of truth, great in the possession of a sound
mind, great in her power of framing the future of her
children, as they behold every day the nobleness of her
own character, as she almost unconsciously imprints
upon them that self-reliance, which is worth more
than gold, that honour which is above suspicion. He
who leaves such a home to fight life's battle, takes with
him a heritage the proudest he can possess. While
such a mother is seen "looking well to the ways of her
own household, and eating not the bread of idleness,
her children rising up and calling her blessed her husband, also, and he praising her;" how can one help ex-

claiming "Many daughters have done virtuously, but thou excellest them all." It rests with the mothers to say what our merchants will be ; whether they are to exhibit those qualities which make them successful, or those which render success impossible. Wills have to be broken, restraints have to be imposed, self-denial learned, perhaps painfully ;—all these lessons have to be taught him by a mother who fully comprehends how essential they are to his future, and intelligently understood by the boy before he has finished that education which will enable him to go forth into life. Mothers who pamper their boys, who encourage them in an expenditure which can ill be afforded, which can beget only habits of idleness, extravagance and pride, who cannot think of having them do what their fathers had to do, are ruining them. They do not think so, I know, but they are ; and that poor, dear boy of yours, (we may say to a many a mother,) who is so good, and so gentle, and so kind, and who knows so little of the world (although he knows vastly more of it than you think he does) has been unfitted by you (with the best intentions I have no doubt), yet by you, for that station in life which he might have filled with credit had his training been different ; and who, unless he be taught, and that speedily, that there are fields in which he may win greater distinction than in hanging about his mother's skirts ; unless he go out into the world and prove himself a man, he will become an incubus on society, and so far as any practical benefit he is every likely to be to any one, beyond some fancy hair dresser, or going to evening parties, he might just as well be put in a band-box, and allowed to remain there. There are hundreds of young men among us, and some who are no longer young, who are suffering life to pass away in unbroken dreams of what "the governor" is going to do for them. While others will tell you with the greatest seriousness, that they have a rich old aunt either in Ireland, or elsewhere, or some other relative at whose decease they will be "made" for life. They tell you this with an earnestness which would lead you to believe that no tidings would give them greater pleasure than those of the death of the kind friend by whom they expect to be remembered. Send your boys out into the world, let them become familiar with its rough side. Let them make their own mark. Teach them to be noble, self-reliant and true.

Be careful of your expenditure ; every dollar you withdraw from your business needlessly is a thrust at your success. It is like taking away an effective man in presence of the enemy. It is worse; it is like taking an effective man and handing him over to the enemy. Some wonder why the end of the year finds them no better off than they were at its beginning. There have been large sales, fair profits, but no addition to capital. There need be no mystery. They indulged in everything their fancy led them to desire. This because it was a trifle, that because they wanted to be like some neighbour, and something else because they wanted to surpass another. The temptation all the stronger because these matters, whatever they might be, had not to be paid for for several months. These people never know what it costs them to live ; an account they never keep ; self-denial they do not understand. Could you get them to keep an account just for twelve months (but you could not), of all the money spent upon trifles, you would startle them, though we fear you could not cure them, for in business or out of business, such persons never succeed. They pass through life making no headway, and when age comes upon them, it finds them without provision for its infirmities.

Be careful of your time. Time is money ; husband it well ; let it be understood that, when men look for you in business hours, you are to be found. You cannot afford to be gossiping with others, or have others coming to gossip with you. Many a man has been ruined by that readiness which leads him to attend to every one's business but his own, neglecting to attend to his own fortune, as he busies himself with the affairs of others, to be pitied at last for his pains. In every community it is the simplest possible thing to put your finger upon scores of just such men.

Be careful of your companions. If you want to succeed, the theatre, the saloon, the gambling hall, are not the places for you. He would not be a prudent merchant who would open accounts with young men, knowing them to be frequenters of such places. Don't seek companions who can only corrupt, while you can find so many who can profit.

Don't engage in work that is hurtful, when you can find so much that is elevating; the world is full of work in which you can be helpful to your fellows:

> " Lives of great men all remind us
>   *We* can make our lives sublime,
> And, departing, leave behind us
>   *Footprints* on the sands of time.

> *Footprints* that perhaps another,
>   Sailing o'er life's solemn main,
> A *forlorn* and *shipwrecked brother*,
>   *Seeing*, shall take heart again."

You can find, in the work in which this and kindred Associations is engaged, enough to occupy the time you may have to give, enough to call forth the talent you pos-

sess, you will find among the workers in such Associations congenial spirits, whose friendship may not only be
profitable, but life-long, and all the more endearing because found in connection with work so elevating ; and
thus from the first you may shew that it is possible to do
well for both worlds, to be "diligent in business, fervent in
spirit, serving the Lord."

Young men have found their account sometimes
suddenly closed, forgetting that the banker or the mer
chant could forsee that the money spent at the saloon,
the gaming table, and at the livery stable for fast horses,
could have one end only, and that end ruin—not of business only, but of mind and body. They felt that in
opening the account they made a mistake, they decide,
however, to make a present loss, rather than afford an
opportunity of making it greater, and so close the account. If you want to be successful, be careful of your
companions.

Be careful of your character. "A good name
is rather to be chosen than great riches.—*Prov.* 22, i.
Character, like a shadow, accompanies all men, and
whether good or bad, it cannot be shaken off. A father
who leaves to his son a good name, and that only, leaves
him a priceless inheritance ; one which will never fail
him if fully appreciated and properly improved.

Love the truth. Let nothing move you from it, for no earthly consideration swerve from it, suffer loss if it must be, but speak the truth. Never equivocate; never give an answer to mislead, or an answer that you know misleads; never take advantage of your reputation for truthfulness to promote your own ends by framing your speech so as to have the semblance of truth while in your heart you know you are misleading; such conduct is more reprehensible than glaring falsehood, and though you may thus gain a temporary advantage, rest assured that upon no such foundation can you erect a successful business.

Be careful of the interest of your creditors; if you are anxious that no one should lose by you, you begin with the best incentive to success. So long as you are thus influenced, you are furnished with one of the best safe guards against failure. Credit is capital; do not abuse it. You have secured it possibly more on account of your character than your means. So long as you maintain it unimpaired, it is a fortune; *be careful of it.* Feel that your first duty is to discharge your obligations, to divert into unwarranted channels *not one dollar* which should be applied in reducing them. Your capital puts you in possession of means, if you waste the one, rest assured you will destroy the other.

4

The man who relies upon a credit to enable him to carry on his business may be called I know a dependent man, and yet I fancy that if business were reduced to an absolutely cash basis, many large and healthy concerns in the old world, and in this new one, would find themselves suddenly pulled up. But admit that the man who does conduct his business on a credit derived from the merchant or banker, is a dependent man. It has been so ordered that every high-minded man does experience just in that state, a pleasure and a satisfaction as great as he is ever after likely to know, no matter how great the volume of his business or the extent of his means. Nothing can give greater pleasure to a high-minded business man than to discharge his obligations ; and in doing this he is affording his creditors the best evidence he can give them that their confidence has not been misplaced. But he is doing more than this, even though a humble trader, he tends by every such transaction to strengthen and uphold public credit. He leads even the doubtful man to put confidence in his fellow man, he leads those who look at balance sheets only as actuaries, to feel satisfied that, although the crisis may come, and may bring with it much suffering, and much loss, that with men thus careful of their credit, who thus look upon their obligations as sacred, the crisis may be severe, and may be wide-spread, but it cannot be universal.

Do not be restless because you have to do your business upon credit, so long as you feel you have never abused it, or intend to do ; so long as you are conscious that you are worthy of it, and intend to be ; so long as you feel that it is a benefit, not only to yourself, but to those who bestow it. You occupy a good position, a proud position, one that will afford you as much pleasure as you are ever likely to know, throughout your entire business career, and while the man who is constantly straining his credit to the utmost limits, and ever calling give! give ! has it continued with doubt, if indeed it is not curtailed or stopped, yours will be increased, as your business requires its expansion, and that to the mutual advantage of your creditors and yourself.

When the crisis comes, and when men who have much at stake look over their assets, and as name after name passes under their eye, the question is not so much what a man has, but what he is ; not what his means, but what his character. Is he truthful? Will he equivocate? Will his assets be found to be the property of his father-in-law, or of some creditor trumped up for the occasion ? or will he be one who has nothing to hide, but will be found on that, as upon every other occasion, clear as the noon day ?

This carefulness, while it will inspire you with fortitude, will lead you to avoid all speculations ; will lead you to be satisfied that at nothing will you make so much, or do so well, as at your own business. A miner sometimes stumbles upon an immense nugget of gold, or one may find a diamond of enormous value ; but that the value of either gold or diamonds are not affected by such occurrences, is good evidence that they are but accidental. So with speculation ; one man in ten thousand, reckless enough to employ in some wild enterprise the means entrusted to him for his business, may come out safe ; but where he does, more than one thousand will fail. The young man who, in Wilmington, not long since, helped a feeble old man over a street-crossing, was engaged in active business; that act was but the outcropping of his own goodness of heart. Soon after he found himself very unexpectedly remembered in the old man's will to the extent of Forty Thousand Dollars. He had already found his reward by contributing to the old man's comfort; the legacy was an unexpected reward, though not a richer one than the other. But the young men who make it their business to wait at street crossings to help feeble old men over, that they may be remembered by them in their wills to the extent of Forty Thousand Dollars, will have to wait a very long time—as they deserve to do.

This carefulness will lead you statedly to take your

stock and balance your books. Which of us would feel safe with a captain who neglected taking his daily obser- vations; nor with such a captain would we be surprised to find ourselves among the breakers. You may regard it as a safe rule that the man who does not take some method of periodically ascertaining his position, is not likely to make a successful business man.

This carefulness will lead you judiciously and con- stantly to insure your property. It is simply amazing how many men are ruined by the neglect of this simple matter; not in terribly desolating fires merely, but in fires which happen throughout the year in our towns, villages and cross roads. Men who obtain a credit should feel it to be a duty incumbent upon them to insure their property against loss by fire. This carefulness leads many to insure their lives. The husbanding of the means for the payment of the premiums is itself a discipline of the most healthful character to every beginner, while the thought that he does this to promote the welfare of those he may leave behind him, and to make his creditors yet more safe, enables him with a lighter heart and a firmer purpose to push his business.

This carefulness will make you *cheerful.* Many a man has failed in business through his manner; has been unconscious of the cause, and had no friend honest enough to tell him the truth. A man who has a monopoly of a commodity which people want, and must have, and which they can obtain only from him, may be as gruff, and as uncouth and as surly as he pleases, without affecting his income. But where men have to deal in commodities the very same as hundreds of competitors have to offer, bought as well, held in quantities as large and qualities as good, they will go to the man whose face has the most sunshine and who serves them most pleasantly. And you cannot blame them. There are some men, and good men too, and honest men, yet they pass through life as though no pleasant sunbeam had ever shed its soft light across their countenance, and who have never learnt the important lesson, that true suavity of manner is an important element in a man's business success.

A Rothschild or a Baring may assume a stiffness or an indifference of manner without injury to themselves, which would simply be fatal to any young man who had his business to make. To one of the Rothschilds a German prince brought letters of credit; he was shown into the inner room of the famous banker, whom he found busy with a heap of papers. On his name being announced the banker nodded, offered his visitor a chair, and went on with his work. The prince, who felt that everything should give way to one of his rank and dignity, was not prepared for this treatment, and, standing, said, " Did you not hear, sir, who I am ?" repeating his titles. " Oh ! very well," said Rothschild, " take two chairs then." Until you become a Rothschild or a Baring, a little more attention will be expected on the part of those who bring letters of credit to you ; and you never will become either the one or the other, nor will you ever be possessed of the means or influence of many men found in grades far below such commercial giants, unless you impress the mind, not of a prince merely, but of your humblest patron (who may one day become a prince), that, in doing business with you, he confers as great a favour upon you as you can possibly confer upon him. Whatever a man's position, it costs little to be courteous to all. The constant exercise of this quality will minister immensely to his own happiness in passing through life, while it will greatly contribute to the happiness of others.

As soon as you can afford it (not before), get married. No companion can be so helpful to you in every respect as a good wife. No spot in this world should have such attractions for you as your own home, made comfortable by your own industry, and gladdened by the smiles of those who love you.

Young men should marry as early as circumstances will warrant, as one of the best means of saving them from numberless snares, and securing their happiness and prosperity. Marry in your own station ; don't wait until you have amassed a fortune, that you may look for the hand of some Nabob's daughter, possibly to be refused ; when the sympathies of youth no longer remain, and when such a marriage, even if practicable, could be but one of policy or convenience. You can always find among your own friends those quite as good as yourself, and whose sympathies and associations, being like your own, afford the best evidence that your life will be a happy one. It is as true to-day as it was when written by the wise man, that "Whoso findeth a wife findeth a good thing."—Prov. xviii. 22.

Be enthusiastic. From the moment of your beginning, let your motto be *forward!* Be determined to be successful, or the probabilities are you will fail. Inspire every one about you, as far as that is possible, with your own earnestness, cheerfulness and truthfulness. Place every man in your employment in the position for which he is best fitted. Keep no drones about you ; have no unfaithful men about you ; no eye-servants who, though making their bread from your business, are neither true to its interests nor to you.

Be the mainspring of your own business, the con-
trolling and directing power which keeps the whole in
constant and harmonious motion ; impress every one
around you that you are a thorough master of your own
business, able to guide your vessel in the tempest as in
the calm ; that difficulties but inspire you with greater
earnestness to achieve greater results. Take an interest
in every one in your employment; an interest in their
comfort, welfare and happiness. Give them your confidence ; don't suffer faithful services to go unrewarded.
In addition to what you promise to pay them, let them
feel that they, as well as you, have a direct pecuniary
interest in the development and extension of your business, and that the more they are able to make for you
the more will they make for themselves.

Advertise your business. Better, however, a hundred times, never do so, than do it untruthfully. If it
be true that not more than five men out of every hundred
succeed, make up your mind to be one of them, if but
one of that five, take the highest commercial position ;
try for it. Do not expect to escape without detractors.
There never was a successful man, and there never will
be, who had not and who will not have his enemies.
The envious will look on and say, with apparent sin-
cerity, that they hope this will not end in disaster, while

nothing would give them more pleasure than your failure. There will be those who, while speaking fairly to your face, would damage your credit if they could. But there is a power in the really earnest, progressive man, which bears down the combined assaults of envious and spiteful men. Never mind them; go on. What though they call you mean, as perhaps they will; over-reaching and unprincipled, as possibly they may; go on, extend your business upon sound and honourable principles, and every hour you will increase the distance between yourself and your traducers ; and as you go up, they will go down. Keep wisely extending your business, making all you can ; and, as you do so, giving all you can. Undertake nothing upon which you cannot ask God's blessing ; do not forget that it is His blessing alone which maketh rich, and addeth no sorrow; and do not forget that all who seek success without it—however large their business, or numerous their friends—will find that, for all their toil and care, they have but gathered for this world and the next, " *Sadly at last, nothing but leaves.*"

So conducting your business, you will have little to fear from the crisis; for although it is certain to bring ruin to thousands, it is almost equally certain to benefit you. The crisis either makes or mars a man. " The

crisis of 1837, which brought ruin upon so many thousands, made George Peabody. Three-fourths of all the
banks in the United States fell with a terrible crash;
thousands of prosperous traders were ruined ; credit for
the time paralyzed ; American securities were worthless.
Amid all this upheaving, Peabody stood firm. In the
parlour of the Bank of England, where not half-a-dozen
men in the kingdom would have been listened to on
American matters, his judgment commanded respect ;
his integrity won back confidence in the securities of his
country. That day, so dark to so many, was the beginning of his greatness, placed him at once in the foremost
rank of merchant princes, gave him unbounded credit,
and ultimately a world-wide reputation ; led to that
splendid career familiar now to every school-boy, to the
amassing of a princely fortune ; to the founding of a noble
charity, which finds homes for the poor of London
without making them paupers—which ministers to their
comfort without causing them to sink their independence ;
and whose name would have lived throughout all time,
even without the statue erected at the Royal Exchange
to perpetuate his memory. "Show me a man diligent in
business, he will stand before kings, and not before
mean men."

Do not be frightened at difficulties ; do not let
disasters overwhelm you.

The history of the Allan Steamship Company is part of our country's history. A Canadian line seemed not only a desirable undertaking, but one urgently demanded by the growing trade of the country. Such a line the Allan Company undertook, and gave it their name. Disaster seemed to attend all its early efforts; ever and anon came the tidings of the loss of well-built ships, and not of ships only, but of brave men; and then came sadder stories still, where ships went down and none were left to tell the tale. Yet the Company went on; some predicted their failure, perhaps wished it; others said the subsidy ought to be withdrawn, and would have withdrawn it, if they could. Yet the Company went on. Ordinary men would not only have quailed before losses less overwhelming, but sank under them. Yet the Company went on; it was their crisis, and it made them; they learnt lessons from disaster, and benefitted by them; improved their steamships, their discipline and management; so perfected their entire system, that their fleet of steamships to-day is as large, as safe and as skilfully managed as any line in the world; while the men themselves are living examples of what can be accomplished by the pluck that refuses to be daunted, and the energy which knows no tiring. Nor is it at all unlikely that those of our Canadian youth, who exhibit like energy and produce like results, may be honoured with marks of royal favour such as those bestowed on the founder of that Company, which not even the envious can grudge, and which all right thinking men will say have been well deserved.

Another illustration, and we have done. No disaster ever fell upon people, during the century, equal to that which fell upon the people of Chicago on the 9th of October of last year. Never did a people in any land rise above disaster with more commendable energy. The burned area extended over two thousand one hundred and twenty-four acres, or nearly three and half square miles; seventeen thousand four hundred and fifty buildings were destroyed; ninety-eight thousand five hundred people were rendered homeless; two hundred and fifty perished in the flames; property amounting to six hundred and twenty millions of dollars was destroyed. To form some idea of the extent of this disaster you may fancy every building in this city swept away, and add to it another city of moderate size. Imagine every man, woman and child in Toronto, Hamilton and Kingston, and nearly three thousand more belonging to some other city, shivering beside the smouldering remains of their dwellings, the homes once not of comfort only, but of opulence; not homeless merely, but destitute of food, clothing and means. Imagine the entire wealth of this city swept away in a few hours by the devouring flames, then multiply that twenty fold, and you will have some idea of the desolation and ruin caused by that terrible conflagration. And then if you were told that that vast company, stripped of all earthly goods, rose up after that night of desolation with a calm settled confidence, with an energy which, appearing to be more than human, refused to be stilled, and which seemed to defy disaster even so appalling. If you were told that such men went forth, with glad trustful hearts, to begin anew life's battle, full of life and full of hope, determined to make their cities of the future greater far than their cities of the past, the whole would appear to you but as some wild fairy tale which you would find it impossible to believe ; yet all this the people of Chicago did.

Four weeks after the fire, and ere its smoke had fully cleared away, the Chicago *Tribune* had this article : " We are once more on our feet ; we have not much to offer in the way of show, architecture, or plate glass. We do not wear good clothes, we are decidedly shabby ; but we have within us an abundance of the same stuff that made the first Chicago a great city. Our credit in all the markets of the world is unimpaired ; our geographical position the same as it was before the fire ; we have as many railways as before ; as many trains running on

them, and all heavily laden ; we have the money in hand
to pay the interest on our city debt ; to rebuild our
burned bridges and our public offices ; we have faith in
God and a heart full of gratitude to the whole world for
its timely assistance in the hour of our calamity, and now
we start again to achieve honourable distinction among
American cities, a trifle crippled, a little hurt, somewhat
untidy in outward seeming ; but still, with unconquered
souls."

That these were not boastful utterances, but the language of men of calm, resolute, settled purpose, may be
gathered from what has actually taken place. On the
18th March, just five months after that desolating fire, the
Chicago *Times* had this article :

" Animation, confidence, prosperity, were the char-
acteristics of the week just closed. On every hand, in
every channel of trade there was a glow of life which
seemed to bid defiance to the disasters of the past. Even
the ruins were all aglow with life, and in each and every
block of the new Chicago, the merry ring of hammer
and trowel kept time to the movement of merchandize
from buildings yet scarcely completed. To-day her trade
is more expansive, her profits larger, her prospects
brighter, than at any other period of her history. The

millions of property swept away in the fire are things
of the past and almost forgotten, and ere the year is old,
will, through the rapid strides of trade, be nearly or quite
recovered."

We might have called your attention to the history
of those who became renowned as business men, whose
characters pure, grand and lofty, might be presented to
you as models in every way worthy of your imitation.
We have chosen rather to call your attention to those
principles which formed the foundation of their greatness.
We have done this because the humblest one in this assembly may adopt them; and, practising them, must be
successful. There are none here who cannot be noble,
virtuous, and true; none who need be either idle or
slothful. Each one may be fired with a lofty ambition to
improve his own condition and minister to the good of
his fellows. Influenced by the principles which have made
our great men great, you will be successful. Yours may
not be a renown as great as that of Peabody. You may
never have the large means, or the large heart, or the large
sphere of the great and good Henry Thornton, of whom
Wilberforce said to Hannah More; " If you undertake
the work of reclaiming and clothing the neglected, I will
find the means, for I have a rich banker in London,
Mr. H. Thornton, whom I cannot oblige so much as in

drawing upon him for such purposes." But if your sphere should not be so large, you will find one ample enough for the profitable employment of your energies, and if your wealth should not be so great, you will have all you need for yourself and others. You cannot all be Wilberforces, or Thorntons, or Peabodys, but you may all be successful. Your future is before you, and it is for you to make it just what you please. In this Dominion you will find a field large enough to task your ability, with rewards abundant enough to recompense you for your toil. You can be the founder of your own business and of your own fortune. It may be yours to take many a brother by the hand in whom you find qualities worthy of encouragement, and help him to shape his future. It may be yours to stand by many a deserving business man in the hour of trial, who but for such assistance would be involved in ruin. Yours to roll away the reproach which unprincipled men bring upon trade. Yours to have , made the world better for your having been in business, yours to leave behind you an imperishable memory, and to have your name inscribed upon that distinguished scroll of your country, upon which is written the names of its great, its good, and its *successful men*. And away down through the long future, in many of our Canadian homes as boys through the long winter evenings, gather around the cheerful hearth to hear the stories of those who from

small beginnings, became great, and useful and good,
the story of your own toils, and your own triumphs,
will often be told ; and, pointing to your own honourable
and prosperous, and it may be, distinguished career, the
father will tell his boys that if they would be successful as
you were, they must battle like you.

www.ingramcontent.com/pod-product-compliance
Lightning Source LLC
Chambersburg PA
CBHW020239090426
42735CB00010B/1761